My CHRISTMAS ACTIVITY Book

Bethan James and Gillian Chapman

The angel's news

Mary was soon to be married to Joseph, the carpenter. But one day God sent the angel Gabriel to tell her a great secret.

'Don't be afraid,' said the angel. 'God has chosen you to have a baby who will be called God's son. His name will be Jesus.'

Mary loved God. She was ready to be the mother of the baby Jesus.

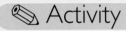 Activity

Circle five differences between the pictures.

 Activity

Which of these angel shapes is the same as the angel above?

a　　　　　b　　　　　c

✎ **Activity**

What was the name of the angel?

G _____ ....

✎ **Activity**

Fill in the missing letters to reveal part of what the angel told Mary?

D	O	N		■	
E	■	A		R	
I		■		O	D
■		A		■	C
H		S	E		■
Y		U	■	■	■

The journey to Bethlehem

The Roman emperor had ordered a census. Everyone had to go to their home town to be counted. Joseph had to take Mary to Bethlehem.

It was a very long, dusty journey and Mary knew that it was nearly time for her baby to be born.

 Activity

Complete these names for the census.

M__ __y

J__ __ __ __h

J__ __ __s

✎ Activity

Can you help Mary and Joseph find the fastest way to Bethlehem?

Start

Bethlehem

No room at the inn!

Joseph knocked on the door of the inn but there were many people in Bethlehem for the census. They had no room.

'You are welcome to sleep in the place behind the inn where the animals sleep. At least the straw is dry and you'll be safe for the night,' said the innkeeper.

It was dark but the innkeeper's lamp lit the area showing the colours of the stable. What colours do you get when you mix the paint colours below?

✎ Activity

1  + =

2 + =

✎ Activity

Complete the sign to show that there are no rooms available?

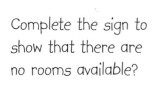

✏️ Activity

How many stars are there in the picture?

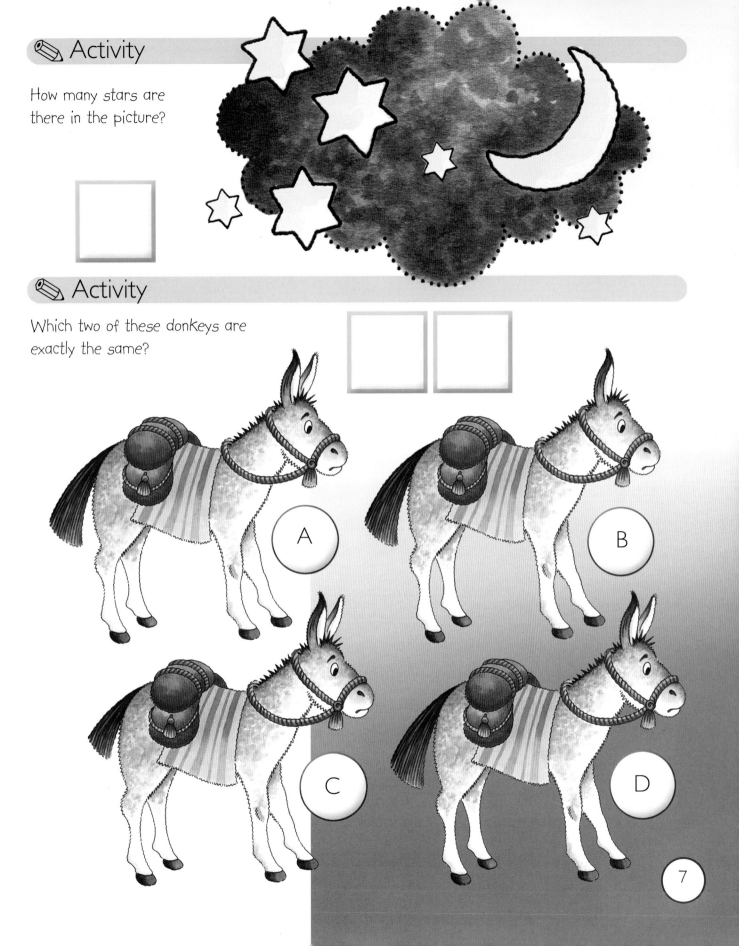

✏️ Activity

Which two of these donkeys are exactly the same?

A

B

C

D

7

Joseph takes care of Mary

Joseph helped Mary inside and made her comfortable. The donkey was nearby and there were other animals in the stable too. But Mary was pleased to rest.

As they waited Mary thought about the angel's message and the baby boy who would soon be born.

Activity

Each of these animals has one thing missing. Draw in the missing part to complete the animal.

1

2

3

Find and circle six differences between the two pictures of Mary and Joseph.

Select the correct answer from this list. Write the answers in the boxes below.

a little sister.   b patient.   c wife.
d animals.   e baby.

1 A vet cares for

2 A mother cares for her

3 A husband cares for his

4 A doctor cares for his

5 A big brother cares for his

4

5

6

7

8

Mary's baby boy

That starry night, Mary gave birth to her baby. They called him Jesus as the angel had told her.

Mary wrapped him in strips of cloth and made a bed for him in the manger.

✎ Activity

Which way up are the picture strips? Tick the strips that are the right way up and cross the strips that are upside-down.

1   2   3   5

4

✎ Activity

What name did Mary give to the baby?

J...................... ....

Where do the puzzle pieces fit?
Put the number of each puzzle piece
in the white box next to the space
where it fits.

Jesus, the baby king

Jesus was a baby king, but he had been born in a stable with the animals looking on. Jesus was the son of God but his bed was a manger full of hay.

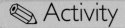 **Activity**

Which one of these details does not come from the picture opposite?

 Activity

Draw three lines to show each of the three matching pairs?

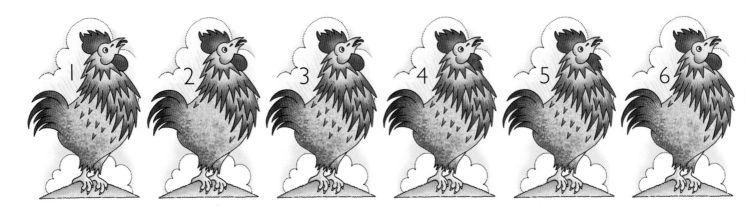

Connect the baby to the manger by drawing a line. Can you do it without touching the red lines?

Activity

Trace over the pale blue lines to complete the picture.

13

Shepherds hear the good news

Shepherds were looking after their sheep that night. Suddenly the whole sky was filled with light.

'Don't be afraid!' an angel said. 'I bring good news of great joy! Today in Bethlehem your Saviour has been born. You will find him lying in a manger.'

✎ Activity

Which of these angels has a problem?.

✎ Activity

1	2	3

4	5	6

Tick the details that are taken from the picture. Put a cross by the details that don't match.

Draw a line through the word ANGEL each
time you *see* it in the box below.
Can you find four angels?

A	A	N	A	A	G
A	N	N	N	N	E
N	A	N	G	E	L
G	L	L	E	E	G
E	A	N	L	E	L
L	A	N	G	E	L

A Saviour in Bethlehem

A great host of angels appeared, singing beautiful songs to God:
'Glory to God in the highest and peace on earth to all people!'
Then the shepherds hurried into Bethlehem looking for a new-born baby. The innkeeper showed them to the place where he kept his animals.

✎ Activity

Draw a line from each of the circles below to the three places in the picture that have changed.

Complete the sentences.

A flock of

S

A host of

A

Write the correct square number in each box to re-create the picture above.

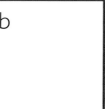

3

4

a	b
c	d
e	f

1

5

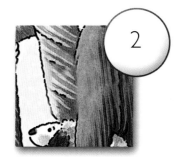

2

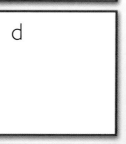

6

The baby in the manger

There the shepherds found Mary and Joseph. There, in a manger, wrapped in strips of cloth, was the new-born baby: Jesus, their Saviour.

The shepherds looked at the tiny baby and felt great joy. They told Mary and Joseph about the angels and their message.

✎ Activity

Draw in the body of the sheep.

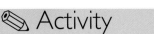

✎ Activity

1 How many sheep are there on the far hill?

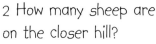

2 How many sheep are on the closer hill?

3 How many sheep are sitting around the shepherd?

Fill in the missing letters to complete
the crossword.

			J	O	S		P	H
H					H			O
R				J		S	U	
I			M					T
			A		H			
T		A	N	G		L		
M					R		O	
			E		D		N	
S	T		R		S			

A very special baby

When Jesus was eight days old, Mary and Joseph took him Jerusalem with two doves as their offering to say thank you to God for their new son.

Simeon had been waiting all his life to see the Saviour whom God had promised to send.

'Lord God, now I may die in peace, for I have seen the one who will bring light to everyone on earth.'

 Activity

Can you follow the path with your pen without touching the lines?

 Activity

Number the picture strips in the right order to re-create the picture.

✏️ Activity

Where do the puzzle pieces fit?
Put the number of each puzzle piece
in the white box next to the space
where it fits.

Wise men in the east

When Jesus was born, some wise men in the east saw a bright new star in the sky.
'Look!' said one. 'A new king must have been born!'
They decided to go to worship the new king.

✏️ Activity

How many different things that you might *see* in the sky can you find?

✏️ Activity

Find the *seven* differences between the two pictures.

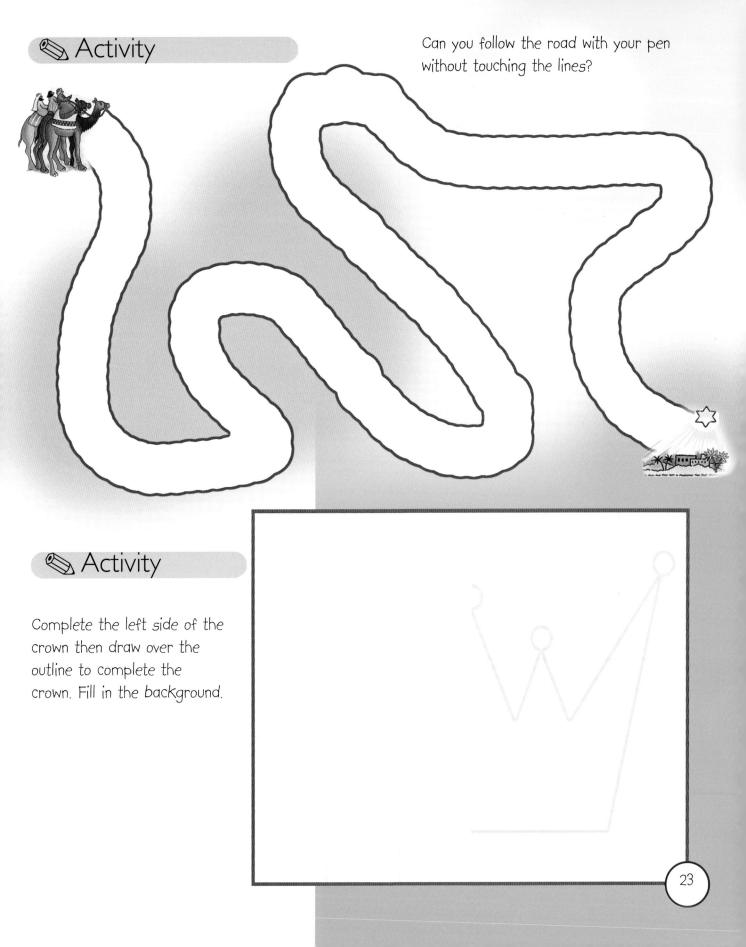

✏️ Activity

Can you follow the road with your pen without touching the lines?

✏️ Activity

Complete the left side of the crown then draw over the outline to complete the crown. Fill in the background.

Following the star

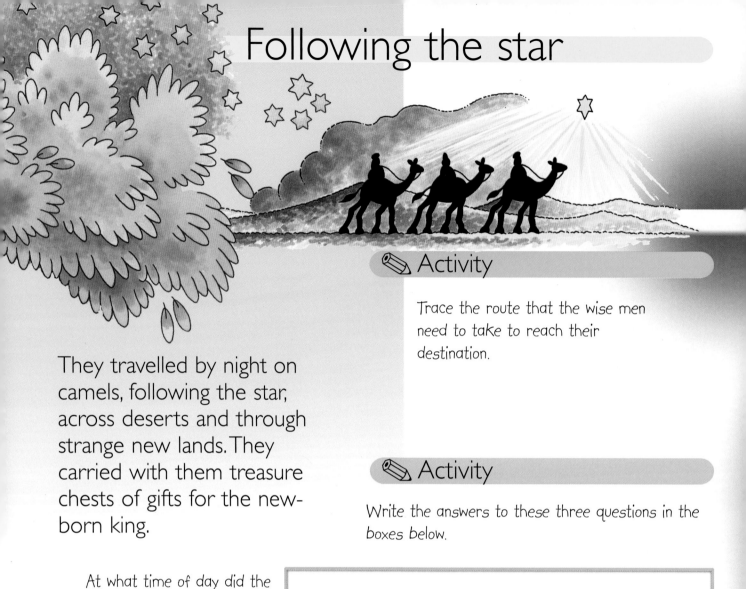

They travelled by night on camels, following the star, across deserts and through strange new lands. They carried with them treasure chests of gifts for the new-born king.

Activity

Trace the route that the wise men need to take to reach their destination.

Activity

Write the answers to these three questions in the boxes below.

At what time of day did the wise men travel?

What did the wise men ride on for their journey?

The wise men travelled from the east, so what direction were they travelling?

✏️ Activity

How many small yellow stars
can you find inside the maze?

25

Jealous King Herod

When they reached Jerusalem, the wise men went to the palace.

'We have come to see the new king,' they said.

King Herod was not happy to hear that there might be a new king – but he called together the chief priests and teachers and asked them where the new king would be found.

'In Bethlehem,' they said.

 Activity

Put a line through the three words that are wrong.

When they reached London, the wise men went to the shops. 'We have come to see the new bargains,' they said.

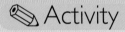 Activity

Tick the right picture to show which face the King pulled when he heard about the new King.

1

2

3

✏️ Activity

Where do the puzzle pieces fit?
Put the number of each puzzle piece in the white box next to the space where it fits.

✏️ Activity

How many flies can you find buzzing around the palace?

Wise men worship Jesus

When the wise men reached Bethlehem, the star seemed to stop above a small house.

There they found Mary, with Jesus on her knee. The men knelt to worship the baby king.

✎ Activity

Join the dots with ten lines to make a star. Colour in the dark sky background.

✎ Activity

Find and circle six differences between the two similar pictures.

28

To re-create this picture the squares have to be put in the correct place. Write the right square number in each box.

✏️ Activity

How many special gifts did the wise men bring for Jesus?

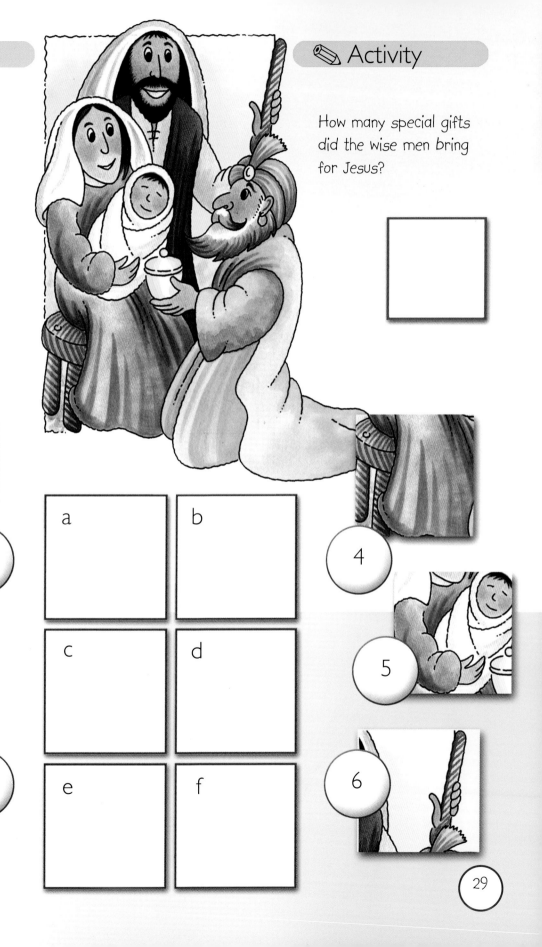

1

2

3

a

b

c

d

e

f

4

5

6

29

Gifts for the baby king

Then the wise men offered him gifts of gold, frankincense and myrrh as Mary watched in wonder.

God warned the wise men in a dream not to return to Herod's palace. And Joseph was warned to take Mary and Jesus to Egypt, where they would be safe from cruel King Herod.

 Activity

Put a line through the three words that are wrong.

Joseph was warned to drive

Mary and Jesus to America,

where they would be safe

from cruel King James.

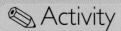 Activity

How many green circles can you find in the picture?

How many blue triangles can you find in the picture?

The wise men brought gifts of gold, frankincense and myrrh to Jesus. Find six things in the wordsearch below that you might give to a baby.

S	O	C	K	S	B
M	F	O	A	N	O
I	A	T	O	A	T
L	R	L	T	P	T
E	A	N	B	P	L
D	U	M	M	Y	E

ANSWERS

Page 2 a

Page 3 Gabriel

Don't be afraid. God has chosen you.

Page 4
Mary, Joseph, Jesus.

Page 5
There are 15 dead ends

Page 6 1 green, 2 orange

Page 7 There are 6 stars

A and D

Page 8 1 feet, 2 body,
3 horns, 4 wing, 5 leg, 6 tail,
7 beak, 8 tail

Page 9
1 d, 2 e, 3 c, 4 b, 5 a

Page 9

Page 10
1 right, 2 wrong,
3 wrong, 4 right, 5 wrong

Jesus

Page 11
1 d, 2 c, 3 e, 4 b, 5 a

Page 12 wrong detail: 3

1 and 3, 2 and 6, 4 and 5

Page 14
1 wrong, 2 right, 3 right,
4 right, 5 right, 6 wrong

Problem angel: 3 (no wings)

Page 15

A	A	N	A	A	G
A	N	N	N	N	E
N	A	N	G	E	L
G	L	L	E	E	G
E	A	N	L	E	L
L	A	N	G	E	L

Page 16

Page 17
a 6, b 1, c 4, d 2, e 3, f 5

sheep and angels

Page 18 1 9, 2 14, 3 7

Page 19:

C			J	O	S	E	P	H
H				H				O
R			J	E	S	U	S	S
I			M		P			T
S			A		H			
T		A	N	G	E	L	S	
M			G		R			O
A			E		D			N
S	T	A	R	S		S		

Page 20
2 5 3 1 4

Page 21
a 5, b 2, c 3, d 1, e 4

Page 22
There are 7 different things

Page 24

night, camels, west

Page 25
There are 11 little stars

Page 26
When they reached ~~London,~~ the wise men went to the ~~shops.~~ 'We have come to see the new ~~bargains,~~' they said.

Picture 1

Page 27:
a 5, b1, c 3, d 2, e 4

6 flies

Page 28

Page 29
a 1, b 6, c 5, d 2, e 4, f 3

3 gifts

Page 30
drive, America, James
7 green circles, 12 blue triangles

Page 31

S	O	C	K	S	B
M	F	O	A	N	O
A	T	O	A	T	O
L	R	L	T	P	T
E	A	N	B	P	L
D	U	M	M	Y	E